The Healing POWER of Purpose

TWENTY-THIRD PUBLICATIONS
185 WILLOW STREET • PO BOX 180 • MYSTIC, CT 06355
TEL: 1-800-321-0411 • FAX: 1-800-572-0788
E-MAIL: ttpubs@aol.com • www.twentythirdpublications.com
Bayard

NOVALIS

Twenty-Third Publications
A Division of Bayard
185 Willow Street
P.O. Box 180
Mystic, CT 06355
(860) 536-2611 or (800) 321-0411
www.twentythirdpublications.com
ISBN:1-58595-273-7

Published in Canada by
Novalis
49 Front Street East, 2nd Floor
Toronto, Ontario, Canada
M5E 1B3
Phone: 1-800-387-7164 or (416) 363-3303
Fax: 1-800-204-4140 or (416) 363-9409
Email: novalis@interlog.com
ISBN: 2-89507-453-4

Library of Congress Catalog Card Number: 2003105417
Printed in the U.S.A.

Contents

What makes our hearts sing? What is that thing that rings a bell in our minds? What makes us smile, count our blessings, and keep going on with our lives?

What makes the things we do every day meaningful? What makes us realize that our lives are fulfilled? Why do we persevere at certain tasks despite many challenges, and yet feel no attraction or zest for other tasks that seem easier?

The answer to these questions may be linked to the choices we make in life. Our lives become meaningful and fulfilling when we respond to a calling instead of the demands of a career, follow a purpose

1

instead of just the requirements of a job, and make a life instead of just making a living.

How privileged are those among us who are able to hear their heart's calling and fulfill what they were meant to do in this life!

When we meet someone for the first time, we have a tendency to introduce ourselves by telling the other person what we do for a living. Am I my job? Are you your job? Of course not. We are much more than what we do. In fact, the opposite seems more accurate: we should do what we are.

Mother Teresa would describe the work of her sisters this way: "The Missionaries of Charity are not social activists but contemplative in the very heart of today's world." Helping people acquire what they need is the job of a social worker. Helping people be what they really are as children of God is a vocation, a calling, a purpose—a powerful healing purpose. It gives meaning to the lives of both the receiver and the giver. Doing good for others is good for you.

There is a passion waiting for you, but you may need to do some homework to find it.

What do you intend to do with your life? Think about it. If you spend, let's say, thirty or forty years being a politician, a lawyer, a teacher, a salesperson, or a machine operator, what will you have accomplished? Does what you do respond to your most profound longing? When you get where you are going, will you be satisfied?

Is being a lawyer God's plan for you? Do you feel that, by being a salesperson with all the money you've made in the bank, you lived really abundantly and truly in the sense of what Jesus said, "I came that they may have life, and have it abundantly" (Jn 10:10)?

Every one of us has a life purpose that is in God's plan. Jobs may come and go, but one never retires from God's plan. It is this very sense of purpose in God's plan that makes everyone unique. If people fail in life, it is very often not because they lack ability, brains, or even the desire to do things, but because they lack a purpose around which they can organize and focus their energies and potentials.

Even though we may work to identify with the purpose that constitutes our destiny, we should keep in mind that life is a journey and we should enjoy the trip. Life is the expression of what we are and we should make it as beautiful as we can.

It would be a wonderful and rewarding gift to me if this little book can make a small contribution to your effort to find the purpose that will allow you to do more and more of what God has in mind for you, and less and less of the other things that stand in the way.

Then, expect wonders.

CHAPTER ONE

Everyone Must Have a Purpose in Life

This one thing I do: forgetting what lies behind and straining forward to what lies ahead.

■ PHILIPPIANS 3:13

Every one of us has a story to tell—an unfolding personal life story. We are what our choices are and, especially, what our driving purpose is. Whatever is happening now is a result of choices we've made in the past, consciously or unconsciously.

We were born with certain talents, characteristics, and a number of qualities and shortcomings. We have intelligence, imagination, and heart. We were, we are, and we become our potentialities, limitations, and all that is in between.

What we can see in the depth of our heart and soul we can materialize in our life.

We are born called, with a mission and a vocation—a purpose. We do what we do with a sense of direction. Martin Buber put it this way: "Direction is that primal tension of the human soul which moves it at times out of the infinity of the possible to choose this and nothing else, and to realize it through action."

We have this sense of "direction," it seems fair to say, even in the midst of contradictory behaviors. In spite of what we see on the surface, the ultimate choice people have in common remains the freedom to be able to be healthy and happy. This means that people want to live up to their fullest potential, fulfill the unique purpose of their life, and live in accordance with their essential nature. And they cannot realize this God-given potential and be—really be—unless they fulfill this purpose.

Furthermore, we are part of the whole purpose of

the universe. "Nature as a whole," says John Dewey, "is a progressive realization of purpose strictly comparable to the realization of purpose in any single plant or animal."

A Sense of Purpose

What we can see in the depth of our heart and soul we can materialize in our life. This seems to be one of the important laws of existence. It is what gives us the energy to realize our uniqueness and, at the same time, to make our contribution to the world.

Loretta was a happy, loving, very sensitive, and sweet child. She was heart-centered. But her circle of family and friends was unbearable. Alcohol, drugs, and violence pervaded much of her miserable environment. Imagine the wounds! Yet she encountered all this with her shy, forgiving, eager-to-please personal nature.

Loretta made mistakes along the way, but she kept going. She succeeded in putting herself through college, then became a talented teacher for over thirty years. The suffering she encountered in her life was enormous. Spiritually, physically, and especially emotionally, she was exhausted. But she was determined to heal herself. She went to psychotherapists. She met

We have a purpose that makes us fully alive.

healers. She frequented spiritual centers. She took the advice of wise people. She associated herself with good and positive friends. The truth is that, underneath her initial confusion and her eagerness to heal, there was a deep longing for recognition, for sharing, and most of all, for connection and love. She wanted to make a contribution—and she did. Without even realizing it, Loretta was a goal-setter.

Whether you know it or not, the universe needs what you, and you alone, have to share. Your contribution makes a difference.

We are born called. We have a special mission and a vocation—a purpose that makes us fully alive. This purpose helps us define our true identity. It helps us move toward our harbor. Otherwise, as Seneca put it, "When a man does not know what harbor he is making for, no wind is the right wind." Montaigne echoed this by saying: "No wind makes for him that hath no intended port to sail unto." With a dream, one sees the invisible and achieves the unbelievable.

We have many impulses, such as to enjoy, to grow, to give and receive, to connect, and to be free. We have many urges—of the body (like breathing), of the psyche (like being moved by an idea or a feeling), and of the spirit (like establishing a relationship with our true self, others, and God). But we are meant to live all these impulses and urges in total integration and in harmonious unity so that what we do reflects what we are, and what we are reflects what we do.

The way we live our life mirrors the values we believe in and the motivations that effect our behavior. There is no doubt that what we hold in the depth of our being tends to be embodied in the open. Therefore, it is of capital importance to pay attention to what we harbor in our minds and hearts. This is even more true when we have defined our purpose in life—no matter what our purpose may be.

We certainly feel that there must be something more to life than just living day by day. Pablo Picasso said: "I paint just as I breathe. When I work, I relax; not doing anything or entertaining visitors makes me tired.… When a man knows how to do something, he ceases being a man when he stops doing it."

Our life has a purpose. We can find this purpose, not by relying on the circumstances that motivate us, but by truly living the reality that most deeply matters to us.

The very reality that matters to us, which makes us happy and continuously longing for the infinite, is not accidental to human nature. It is a basic urge rooted in the very constitution of being human, and implanted in our human nature by its author, God. At no moment can human beings reach a point at which they are incapable of knowing more, wanting more, and loving more. Only the Infinite Being can satisfy such hunger and thirst. A purpose helps alleviate this compelling urge.

Furthermore, a purpose has the power to heal spiritual, psychological, and physical wounds. Study after study has shown that people who have a goal in their life are healthier, happier, and live longer. Volunteers, for example, have fewer illnesses than those who have nothing to live for.

In his book *Peace, Love, and Healing*, Bernie S. Siegel affirms, "Whether it's political or personal, a sense of purpose can do wonders for your health." He goes on to complain about physicians who do not emphasize enough the importance of purpose in the very process of healing: "Physicians are too rarely aware of their patients' need for purpose and meaning in life, so they often don't know how to account for dramatic improvements in their patients' conditions. However, I know there's always a life story behind the change, some kind of existential shift."

We can even go as far as to say that, in a sense, our beliefs become our biology because they have the power to determine moods, and moods alter hormonal activity and immune function. Research suggests that positive thinking—high purpose, altruism, confidence, optimism—has positive effects on our physical and mental health.

> A sense of purpose can do wonders for your health.

Hospitals and clinics are confronted every day with people who are seriously ill. Some of them wish to live, while others want to die. Why do those who are optimistic, and who happen to have the same symptoms that the pessimistic have, live while the others die? The Greek philosopher Socrates answered this question about 2500 years ago by saying: "There is no illness of the body apart from the mind."

In his book *The Wonder of Man*, Dr. Joseph Krimsky echoed Socrates: "It has been demonstrated scientifically that emotional tensions, emotional stresses and strains, may produce chronic depression and fatigue with the lowering of bodily resistance to infection and disease. Prolonged anxiety and worry, uncontrolled passion and temper, the high pressure and tempo of present-day life will bring on degenerative changes in the heart, kidneys, liver and other vital organs, together with hypertension and arteriosclerosis. Hate and fear can poison the body as much as any toxic chemicals."

Robert Ornstein, Ph.D., and David Sobel, M.D., confirm this conclusion in their book *The Healing Brain*: "Our cells can change their activity to conform to the messages which are continually being received from ourselves and others."

> A purpose can keep a person alive when nothing else will.
>
>

At the deepest level, a purpose frees us. By enabling us to see what really matters and focus on what we really love, our purpose helps us to dedicate ourselves to something larger than ourselves. Imagine, then, how many negative emotions and outcomes can be prevented, especially the ones that can cripple us with resentment, anger, jealousy, selfishness, and depression.

A purpose can keep a person alive when nothing else will. Retirement can be the end of a life or the beginning of a new life. All depends on the choices we make. It is true that weight, heredity, diet, and lifestyle are factors for longevity, but Dr. George E. Burch of the Tulane University School of Medicine insists that "the quickest way to the end is to retire and do nothing. Every human being must keep an interest in life just to keep living."

Doesn't this seem obvious when we take a look at the people who live around us? With nothing to live for, no purpose, people deteriorate and degenerate, fast. As Henri Nouwen wrote, "He who thinks that he has finished is finished. Those who think they have arrived have lost their way."

Our Purposes

Our purposes can be primary, secondary, or fundamental. A primary purpose relates to a major result in our life. For example, we can find purpose by working in a meaningful job, possessing a house where we can truly feel at home, or enjoying a constructive and fulfilling relationship. This is what we really want.

The steps to get there are called secondary purposes. The research we do before finding that meaningful job, or that house, or that relationship is the series of steps we take that lead to what we really want as a primary purpose.

Although a primary purpose can eventually become a secondary purpose that allows us to go further and further, it remains nevertheless an end unto itself. When a writer writes a book, the primary purpose is the completion of the book rather than a stepping stone in the writer's career. All depends on how one looks at it. When something is designed to bring some further result, it is a secondary purpose. When the result is clear and one is not aiming further, it is a primary purpose.

Often it is hard to decide whether a purpose is primary or secondary. But this is not really important. What is important is the fact that there is a tremendous power in what we consider as a primary purpose, because we usually rearrange and reorganize our life in ways that help effect the result we are seeking. When we have a primary purpose, somehow this primary purpose will generate the energy to use all the stepping stones of the secondary purposes that lead to the needed result. Every action we take in that direction contributes to building momentum toward achieving our goal.

Why do things happen this way? It is because of our mystical participation. Modern science—physics, chemistry, genetics, biogenetics, as well as the other medical and behavioral sciences—open our eyes to the invisible forces beneath our physical reality.

As Margaret J. Wheatley wrote in her book *Leadership and the New Science*, "The space that is everywhere, from atoms to the sky, is more like [an invisible medium], filled with fields that exert influence and bring matter into form." As Joseph Campbell believes, beyond the archetypal stories by which we usually live our lives, there is an invisible plane supporting the visible one. All this echoes what St. Paul wrote: "What is seen was made from things that are invisible" (Heb 11:3).

Also, things happen this way because our subconscious mind tends to attract whatever it has concluded that we really want. The subconscious mind does not think on its own, does not use logic or reason, and does not abide by moral judgment. It just draws conclusions from what we entertain all day long, what we suggest, and what we are obsessed with. Therefore, when we have a clear primary purpose, we are sending a clear message to the subconscious mind, which takes it as instruction, direction, and input. The subconscious mind does not contest the message. It always says "Yes" to what we direct to it.

If the subconscious mind does not respond properly to a message, that is because we may be sending it contradictory suggestions or because the message is not clear. For example, if someone says, "I really want to write a book. But what I want doesn't make a difference. I never get what I want anyway," this person most likely won't be able to write a book because the subconscious mind is receiving a confusing message. We must send the subconscious mind a strong, clear, and unmistakable message of the result we want, and convince it of the fact that we mean business. This is exactly what a primary purpose does.

Basically, the subconscious mind carries out the goals and objectives that have been sent to it by the conscious mind. On this matter, Jesus Christ, who manifested all the depths of grace and human nature, gave us wonderful insights on how our thoughts can influence our physical circumstances. He repeated this message many times: "If you have faith…nothing will be impossible for you" (Mt 17:20–21), "Whatever you ask in prayer, believe that you have received it, and it will be yours" (Mk 11:24), "All things can be done for the one who believes" (Mk 9:23), "Whatever you ask for in prayer with faith, you will receive" (Mt 21:22).

To let your subconscious mind be your best ally and work to your advantage, a few conditions must be met:

- Set a definite goal with a definite plan to achieve it.

- Believe in your goal and picture it as already achieved. Do not procrastinate.

- Develop strong confidence in yourself.

- Be persistent despite the obstacles you encounter. Never give up. Keep going, going, going. "Victory," said Napoleon Bonaparte, "belongs to the most persevering."

- Do not compare yourself with others.

- Follow Göethe's advice: "Whatever you can do, or dream you can do, begin it. Boldness has genius, power, and magic in it."

When we know what we precisely want, we have a vision of it. Our purpose becomes making this vision a reality. Our purpose gives us a picture of ourselves, and our behavior is bound to match that picture. The way we move from where we are to where we want to be is by using secondary purposes such as making the necessary steps that lead to our goal.

If one's purpose is to write a book, for example, one should devote time for serious research and for writing at least a few pages every day, no matter what, and do anything that helps enhance the writing, such as joining a writers' group or discussion groups and reading relevant books and articles.

At another level, a certain creative tension is also necessary. The goal we envision in front of us and the reality of the present moment create a tension in our consciousness. This is a good and creative tension because it helps us move from where we are to where we want to be. If we are able to increase this tension, we will most likely achieve our goals more quickly. But if we decrease it, we run the risk of not getting what we truly want.

To use all the benefits of this creative tension, we should re-educate our subconscious mind by sending it a message of truth about ourselves: a clear and very accurate report about precisely where we are now and precisely what we want to be. By doing so, we not only have our objective in focus, but we also mobilize the vast number of external and internal resources that are available to us in our endeavor.

In any case, the truth is that what we want to be is in our very hands unless, of course, we inadvertently confront some misfortune. In general, what we see is what we will be. God made us co-creators. Thus, we have the power to create our journey through life.

Our purpose and our determination make things happen. Our purpose keeps us going until we reach our goal. Then we can say, "The world now is a manifestation of the thoughts I had before."

Change the way you think, and you change your world. Virgil put it this way: "They can do all because they think they can." The spirit of your passionate determination, which is a sign of God's will for you, makes things happen the way you want them to happen. Believe you can change your life, and you will. And please keep in mind that the only person who prevents you from doing what you want is you. No one else should be blamed. So, get out of your own way. And as James Allen wrote:

Change the way you think, and you change your world.

> Dream lofty dreams,
>   and as you dream you shall become.
> Your vision is the promise of what
>   you shall one day be.
> Your idea is the prophecy
>   of what you shall at last unveil.

See it. Believe it. Live it.

Moving Ahead

Some people don't move ahead unless they feel comfortable with the move; that is to say they do not move beyond what they already know. They seem to want total security and assurance. This is, of course, understandable.

With a clear purpose in mind, however, people are able to stretch their "comfort zone," to extend their boundaries and move to the next step of their journey, keeping their minds open to new challenges and experiences. Nothing seems able to stop them.

Horace said: "Neither the rage of his fellow citizens commanding what is base, nor the angry look of a threatening tyrant, can shake the upright and determined man from his firm purpose." When a purpose is strong and clear, it becomes like a light that is so bright it completely penetrates our being, guiding us surely in successive steps toward our goal, and dissolving the shadows of doubts and hesitancy. If we dare to genuinely believe in the true purpose of our nature, we cannot afford to stagnate. If we don't go forward, we are sentenced to go backward.

Here are some useful guidelines you may want to consider in setting goals that help in your effort to move ahead:

• Be realistic. You cannot grow wings and you know it. Set goals that are in accord with your nature. Challenging, not utopian, goals are excellent.

• Let your goals be specific and in the present tense, and accept them as if they are already here. Don't say: "It is good to have a healthy lifestyle." Say: "I am living a healthy lifestyle," and mean it.

• Stick with a precise time when it comes to achieving your goals. Don't say: "I have to cook healthy food for my family." Say: "Today, at 9:30 A.M., I am going to the store to buy healthy, organic food so that I can cook a healthy lunch and dinner for my family."

• Always use the affirmative form for your goals. Avoid saying: "I am not going to smoke any-more." Say: "I am free, now and always, of the smoking habit."

• Let your goals be based on truth and positive emotions, never on false motivations, envy, jeal-ousy, or resentment.

For Your Reflection & Response

1. Montaigne wrote in his *Essays* (1580-88): "The great and glorious masterpiece of man is to know how to live with purpose." Elsewhere, he also wrote: "The soul that has no established aim loses itself." Have you ever thought about how important a purpose is in life? Have you ever thought about the "know-what" philosophy as well as the "know-how" philosophy, and how important it is for human fulfillment?

Do you plan your life as if you will live for a long time? Do you schedule your day as if you were about to die? If you had your life to live again, what would you have changed? What are you telling yourself in your thoughts and by your actions? Is what you want in the future consistent with what you are telling yourself now?

2. How do you react to obstacles? Aggravations? Frustrations? Unwanted situations? Your own mistakes? Things that are not going the way you wish? I invite you to compare your answers to what Leonardo Da Vinci said: "Obstacles cannot crush me/ Every obstacle yields to stern resolve/ He who is fixed to a star/ does not change his mind."

3. Some people have a wrong idea about what makes them truly happy. They think that the more self-gratification they can have, the happier they are. Then they realize that only a worthy purpose gives them the fulfillment they were hungry for. Do you agree with this approach? Have you experienced something similar? Do you see a connection between happiness and a sense of purpose?

4. Why is it that when we connect with others, we usually are healthier? No man or woman can live for themselves alone. Consider the statement "No man is an island." We must have some purpose in life outside ourselves. Imagine yourself for a moment completely rejected by everyone, not having one person to turn to, not even to share a confidence or a joke with. Then, imagine yourself for a moment completely immersed in a circle of a happy relationship with family and friends. Compare these two situations.

5. We seem to be busy people, and we seem to want to prove our worth by our busyness. In a sense, a busy life is an indication of a purposeful life. Is this true in general? Is this true in your

own life? Can a very busy life mean sometimes that we don't have a plan for what to do next? Can a busy and well-organized person find time for others? Does a purpose in your life make you feel so busy that you don't have time for anything else, or rather, does it help you be more available?

AFFIRMATION
Repeat this several times a day.
I choose to be healthy.

PRAYER

Dear Lord, your apostle Paul wrote, "This one thing I do: forgetting what lies behind and straining forward to what lies ahead" (Phil: 3:13). This echoes what you said yourself: "If you have faith…nothing will be impossible for you" (Mt 17: 20–21), and "I came that they may have life, and have it abundantly" (Jn 10:10).

This is precisely what I want: to look ahead, dream the unthinkable, have faith in the unbelievable, and do the impossible. I want to live your abundance.

Help me to be healthy, happy, and holy—to live life abundantly. Help me to forget my past, my clinging, my clutter, my wounds, and all that constitutes my false self, and "lose [my] life" in order to "save it" (Lk 9:24).

Help me to move beyond what blocks my path and unlock the mysteries of your purpose for me—my purpose.

I entrust all myself to you. Then, I am sure, I will have greater understanding of you, of myself, and of others. Your way is the way. I will follow.

With you guiding me, I feel renewed in purpose. Amen.

CHAPTER TWO

How to Find Your Purpose

Where your treasure is, there your heart will be also.

■ MATTHEW 6:21

We co-create our own reality. Through sound purposes we create sound reality. A purpose energizes our will, animates our intention, engages our attention, and directs our efforts.

Our purpose is more than a thing we use, a place we reach, a job we perform, or a title we earn. Our purpose does not deal with the role we play in life, but with

26

the way we live our life. In fact, it has the power to define our life and shape our reality—what and who we are. We craft our world. In a sense, our perception of the world becomes our world.

We learn skills. We learn how to read, how to write, and how to follow a map. We are shown how to go from point A to point B. We are shown how to get what we want. But very often we don't know what it is we want. And this is what leaves us behind sometimes, and stuck. Then what do we do? What do we do when we don't know what we want? What do we do when we don't know what we are to do?

Søren Kierkegaard wrote in his *Journal*: "The thing is to understand myself, to see what God really wants me to do; the thing is to find a truth which is true for me, to find the idea for which I can live and die." How do you find that "idea" for which you can live and die?

Guidelines for Finding Your Purpose

There are many ways that lead to finding your own purpose in life. Here are some guidelines:

1. *Pray and listen to God.* Prayer puts you in direct communication with God. Listen to what God is telling you in silence, through others and events, and through God's gifts to you. If your purpose is

> **A purpose energizes our will and directs our efforts.**

not clear, God will make it as clear as you can handle. Learn to sense God's will for you through "what is." Pray again and again, and believe that what you pray for is happening. Jesus said: "Whatever you ask for in prayer, believe that you have received it, and it will be yours" (Mk 11:24).

2. *Make Scripture a reference to your thoughts and actions.* You can be inspired, as many people have been inspired before you, by the word of God. Meditate over it, and let it speak to your mind and heart.

3. *Be aware of the tradition of the Church and stay in touch with God's special witnesses.* The living tradition of the Church and the advice of God's witnesses will open before your eyes horizons you never thought possible, provide directions for dealing with life's challenges and your particular circumstances, and help correct the missteps that have been made.

4. *Tell yourself the truth about yourself.* Know exactly where you are in life. Socrates's famous

dictum, "Know yourself," keeps resonating through the centuries. Know your qualities as well as your shortcomings. Don't hide anything from yourself.

From where you are, you can go anywhere you wish to go. But, how can you get to where you wish to go if you are not clear about where you are? So tell yourself the truth, and the whole truth. You can achieve your goal from where you are if your attitude is right. What you are and who you are matter much more than where you are.

5. *Focus on your soul's desire.* See if you can feel a deeper kind of soul desire, a desire to use your special God-given talents for the benefit of the world, a desire to express your creativity, to share your love for others, and to make the contribution that makes you feel really fulfilled.

"What I do is me: for that I came," wrote Gerard Manley Hopkins. Albert Einstein, who even as a teenager was dreaming about mathematics and theoretical physics, wrote: "That is quite natural; one always likes to do the things for which one has ability." Thoughts coming from your true self create what they aim to create—your true happiness. And don't forget to count your blessings, every one of them, and every day of your life. Blessings are God's special language to you.

6. *Master the great tools of attention and intention.* A true heart's desire holds our attention and intention. And whatever we focus our attention and intention on, we tend to create.

When your attention is fixed on something, your intention will help you cut away distractions by connecting you directly to the object of your attention. Intention is not a kind of a vague wishful thinking. Intention is the arrow that is flying straight to the target.

You can also say that when you intend to do something, your attention is usually in high gear. You are awake, vigilant, and alert. Attention and intention help you discover what you want and they help you get there.

7. *Gain the support of your subconscious mind.* When your attention and intention are focused on a dream, make sure that this dream is in agreement with what you subconsciously believe. The subconscious mind will usually cooperate with the directions you give it. This

means you should give directions that agree with your dream.

Your subconscious mind must believe in your dream. It will only deliver what you consciously tell it to deliver. So try to reorient your dream by using affirmations. Simple statements mark the subconscious mind in a way that works. Make sure you always impress the subconscious mind in a positive way. Otherwise it tends to create what you worry about rather than what you really want.

> Thoughts coming from your true self create your true happiness.

Another effective way to gain the support of your subconscious mind is to surround yourself with positive reading materials, a healthy environment, and especially, safe and enthusiastic friends who believe in you. Don't burden yourself with non-supportive influences such as jealous or selfish "friendships," and don't align yourself with abusive associations or self-interest groups. Rather, take part in opportunities to meet people who share your interests and beliefs by attending workshops that appeal to you or by participating in spiritual communities whose membership you respect and like. We always do better when supported by understanding and caring positive forces.

8. *Eliminate obstacles.* Leave behind you all kinds of unwanted fears, unrealistic presumptions, useless speculations, secondhand opinions, unhealthy clinging, or the fictitious "reality" presented to you by a biased media.

9. *Know your God-given talents and use them to do what you were meant to do.* You will certainly succeed when you are using your natural abilities—when you are doing what you can do best of all. How fortunate if you go to work happy because you love your job. Then, you can go all the way to the top.

10. *Make a decision and commit yourself to carry it out.* No one can tell you exactly what your purpose is. Only you can spell it out. After all, the "What" in "What do you want?" is made up only by you. It is a decision. Perhaps we can fairly say that it is a decision so powerful that, when deliberately made, everything else should and will follow.

Filmmaker Cecil B. de Mille once said, "The person who makes a success of living is the one who sees his goal steadily and aims for it unswervingly. This is dedication." Abraham Lincoln put it this way: "Always bear in mind that your own resolution to succeed is more important than any one thing."

Creating a Purpose Statement

It's time to get more personal. Please don't panic. Discover your own hidden talents and how you can make a better world for yourself and for others. Know that an increase in awareness always makes life more meaningful.

Please do the following exercise without judgmentalism or wishful "If onlys." Make it fun. No one is going to read what you write about yourself, except you. As John wrote in his gospel, "The truth will make you free" (8:32). Ready? Let's start. Please complete the following sentences:

When I was a child, I wanted to be _a mom, nurse_.

When I was a child, I loved to _play outside read, have quiet write_.

When I was a child, people used to love me for _easy going, kind nature, color, happy child_.

Now I love to _Have silence, read, pray, journal, knit walk_.

Now people love me for _my Kindness / thoughtfullness_

~~My qualities are~~ _Generous, friendly_

I would like to be more _Selfless / detach_

I feel very comfortable when _I am alone_.

I am myself when _I am alone, with my husband + my God._

making my significant mark in life

Time seems too short when _I_.

Doing and being all God calls me to

I lose track of time when _I pray I read_.

I seem obsessed by _Not living an ordinary lf_

I have great joy when _I can give + share to other_

When waiting in lines, I think about _How I can be positive / helpful / to another._

The Love of God

When I am alone in nature, I daydream about _My relationship ¿ God, His goodn._

Tiny Houses / Guitar

Without referring to family, job, or circumstances, when I talk to myself, I talk about _Being my best_

How can I most help others So each

(Jacinta) invited me to (Name) made a difference in my life because _The Catholic church_

I am not afraid to speak my truth when _I see or experience injust_

I am in company of like minded people

I find meaning in my life and in events when _Ask for discernment in pr_

sit in the bl sacrament

My persistent intuitive messages tell me that I am

meant to be _in a community of authentic_ *growing, learning & expanding, being salt & light to the world.*

I am loyal to _my Faith & values_ *making a diff Catholics*

I trust myself when _I am following_ *the guidance of Holy Spirit*

The personal achievements I am most proud of are _____ *since the ones that required great faith & courage*

My full attention goes usually to _whatever I_ *am engaged in at the moment* *parent buying 1st car, a new Home*

Even if I do not get paid for it, I still want to _grow + learn — languages / guitar_ *violin Sing to God.*

After you complete these sentences, you may want to take another look at what you wrote. Please do so. But remain spontaneous and don't analyze too much or philosophize, or rearrange things to look better.

Can you see a purpose forming through the answers you have given to the questions above? You may discover that your purpose is different from what you had thought it would be. In fact, even though a purpose can be crystal clear, it may also spring from blind spots, confusion, or secrets hidden in our conscious and unconscious minds.

Also, take a close look at the language you used with yourself (by the way, the language you use with others is revealing too). The subconscious mind does not have the capacity to sort what is true and what is not. It takes every word you say as truth and stores it there.

At this point, and considering all your completed sentences that truly reveal you to yourself, you can make a choice that will constitute the purpose of your life. You know you've done it correctly if you can answer positively the following questions about your stated purpose:

- Does this purpose create in you deep joy and satisfaction?

- Do you feel committed?

- Do you feel that this is you—the real you? Do you feel you want to do it anyway even if you are not paid for it?

Now, write a purpose statement. For example, if you see that part of your calling may be to write a book, start with a statement such as this:

I, Christine, want to write a book. I want this book to be about _____, and it will be titled _____.

Then, set up a timeline, such as this:

I will start writing on _____.

I hope to complete this book by _____.

Then, list the reasons why you chose this purpose.

Identify the risks and obstacles involved, name your anticipated investments and sacrifices in terms of time and money, and note some of the people and organizations that might help you achieve your purpose.

In Christine's case, she should surround herself by things and activities that will motivate her to write: books, journals, group discussions, conferences, and so on.

> The more we become aware of our purpose, the deeper our connection with it will be.

Now, take some time to visualize yourself accomplishing your goal. Christine can visualize herself holding her new book in her hands, reading through its pages, and signing copies for friends or in bookstores. The truth is that the more we become aware of the manifestation of our purpose, the deeper our connection with it will be, and the more it will manifest. By the same token, the more we experience the feeling of using our talents, the more we will attract opportunities to express them.

Visualizing what can be done helps prevent us from being stuck with an unwanted status quo. Every kind of human progress—inventions, medical discoveries, engineering triumphs, business successes or any other successes—were first visualized. Then they became realities. We never get anywhere if we don't know where we are going.

At this point, state your secondary purpose(s) or short-range goal(s). For example:

> I, Christine, will go to the library every day from 12:30 to 2:30 to do the necessary research for the book I am writing.

You need to make a series of short-term goals that lead to the achievement of your primary goal—in this case, writing a book. For all these steps, it is very important to include the following:

• Just start. "The beginning," said Plato, "is the most important part of the work." Do not procrastinate. Start, no matter how difficult the beginning is, and keep going.

• Be specific. State your purpose clearly, unambiguously, and specifically, with time, date, and place when possible. Don't say: "It's important for me to go to the library." Say: "I will go to the library from 12:30 to 2:30 every day." Add a new step every day in the direction of your primary purpose.

• Believe that you can do it. Always remind yourself of what Virgil said: "They can conquer who believe they can."

• Congratulate yourself every time you achieve even the smallest step in the direction of your goal. Share your progress with a friend.

• Find ways to enhance the thoughts, feelings, and actions that lead to your goal.

• Don't let obstacles be a pretext for changing, postponing, or withdrawing from your goal. Keep going in spite of possible setbacks. Persistence is the key to success. If you cannot go fast, go at your own pace. Confucius advises: "It does not matter how slowly you go so long as you do not stop." Also ponder Thomas Edison's wisdom: "Genius is one per cent inspiration and ninety-nine per cent perspiration."

• Avoid negative language, suspend doubts, and keep enthusiasm high.

• Write down your goal and place it where you can see it repeatedly during the day.

• Repeat your goal aloud while driving, playing, working, or waiting in lines. You can even be creative and sing about it when you can!

For Your Reflection & Response

1. Find a quiet place. Sit down. Relax. Take a deep breath. Reflect on the following questions: Have you ever wanted to do something that you never did? What was it? Why didn't you do it? What are the skills you'd like to learn? What aspects of your life do you find yourself committed to?

Are you making a life or just a living? Do you feel that you might still have hidden talents lying dormant? Is there anything you really want to change in the world? Can you give it a precise name? How could you improve the quality of your life in particular and the quality of life in general? Do you live your life according to what you want to change in this world?

2. Take a piece of paper and write your ultimate goal. Say precisely when you want to achieve it. Make a schedule that states time, day, year, and place in which you want to achieve your purpose. Hang this paper in a place where you can see it many times during the day. Follow the schedule you wisely and deliberately established. Henry Ford said: "If you think you can do a thing or think you can't do a thing, you're right." Your feel-

ings and second thoughts should never pull you from your purpose. The only person who can prevent you from doing what you want to do is you.

> Thank God for the beautiful gifts that make you unique.

3. You can find excuses for not being able to follow your purpose. You can blame the circumstances of life and even the weather. If you do that, please stop and regroup. Forget what happened. Start again, and keep moving. Your perseverance and your inner belief in your destiny will lead you to the pinnacle of the achievements that were meant to be and that were designed especially for you.

4. Do you look often to others' purposes and accomplishments? Do you put yourself down when you see others' achievements? Or do these achievements inspire you to strive toward your own achievements?

Do you want to become what you were born to be? Do you think a purpose can be the integrating dynamic of your whole life? Do you think this purpose can help to heal your wounds and contribute to your happiness and holiness? Remember that God will not ask you one day whether or not you became someone else. God will ask you whether or not you became yourself—the person you meant to be.

5. List ten things about yourself that you really like, things like personality, character, skills, and accomplishments. Do you wish your life was different from what it is now? What would you like to change in it? What would you like to maintain and be proud of? Do you thank God for the beautiful gifts that make you unique and that demonstrate the work of the divine grace in your life?

AFFIRMATION

Repeat this several times a day.

With God's grace, I choose to be the architect of my life.

PRAYER

Who am I, Lord?

Why am I so dissatisfied most of the time?

Even though I know I am supposed to be on a journey, why do I feel stuck? Am I not supposed to be in the process of becoming more like you? Am I not supposed to have more of what leads me closer to your divine life, and have less of what drives me away from your holy paths?

I know you have a special and unique plan just for me. Please use me as an instrument of your work here, and grant me the ability to convey your message with as much accuracy as I possibly can. Help me to find a meaning to my life by revealing to me my true purpose, and let the achievement of the purpose be to make the world a better place because you sent me here.

Please, Lord, make of me your faithful, forthright, valiant messenger. Amen.

CHAPTER THREE

Fundamental Purpose

I know the plans I have for you,
says the Lord, plans for your
welfare and not for harm, to
give you a future with hope.

■ JEREMIAH 29:11

With your purpose found and perhaps achieved or in the process of being achieved, you certainly felt great satisfaction—greater than any satisfaction you've ever experienced in your life before. But life is much more complex and mysterious than just moving from point A to point B.

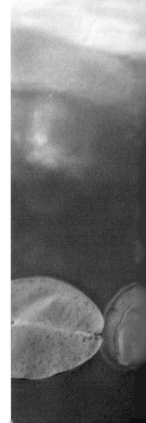

Now you should be at point B. Congratulations!

You are going to realize, however, sooner rather than later, that where you stand at this moment in time is part of an unfolding mystery of human development and spiritual growth. What you've become need not limit where you still need to go. With God you have infinite potential, and your future cannot be limited by your past or by a present status quo.

It is true that you become what you are. But it is also true that you are what you become. We are part of a large movement. We are linked by our whole being—intention, desires, thoughts, actions—to a world much greater than we first realized. We truly are travelers in this life and we can never say we have arrived at our ultimate destination. We may retire from our job or any initial purpose that led us to achieve what we have achieved, but there is no retiring from our fundamental calling and higher purpose.

The passion in us for the infinite explains the presence of God in us, and God's purposes. "The Almighty has his own purposes," said Abraham Lincoln. He also said: "Men are not flattered by being shown that there has been a difference of purpose between the Almighty and them." Albert Einstein was so eager to know God's thoughts that he said: "I want to know God's thoughts…the rest are details."

Higher Purpose

When you found your purpose, you were certainly thrilled, and when you added another achievement to your successful life, you felt on top of the world.

With God you have infinite potential.

The truth is that you found your purpose because you immersed yourself in the bigger picture. This means that the different impulses and passions you had were not chaotic. They were guided by certain patterns and tendencies to go in the direction of the likeness (Gen 1:24) of the one who made them.

Indeed, we are made in the image of God, and this image is alive and active in us. To the question "What is the nature of humankind?" the early Fathers, in contrast to the pagan philosophers, found the answer in divinely inspired words: "Then God said, 'Let us make humankind in our image, according to our likeness'" (Gen 1:26).

As Karl Rahner summarized the view of the early Fathers, this means that "…to be a person is to possess oneself as a subject in conscious, free relation to reality as a whole and its infinite ground and source, God." In other words, God must be the very ground of our being, and our fullest meaning can never be reached unless it is in God's infinite love.

We are created by God, in God, and for God. And this is our true journey: from God to God. Only God knows what human nature is.

We are the living icon of God. The more alive we keep the image in us, the more we become like God. In any circumstance and at any time, we are empowered to mirror God. We mirror God by yielding to Christ. The more we yield to Christ, the more love, which is the essence of our nature, will be the motive of our actions. "Be imitators of God," Paul exhorted his audience, "and live in love, as Christ loved us" (Eph 5:1–2). Even though we cannot reach perfection, we know, however, that God helps us in that direction until the day we can "be like him" (1 Jn 3:2), perfect images of God's love and glory. As the early Fathers put it: "The Divine Word was made man that we might become God."

So let your dream be vast enough to measure up to your God. When you achieve something, be aware of the fact that it is God and others who, in fact, helped you achieve your goal, for the simple reason that your very goal was to reach them. At this depth, you should not set any goal unless your heart is focused on God and others. God said: "I have set before you life and death…Choose life" (Deut 30:19), the life centered in God. That's where the fullness of life ends and also begins. That's where your purpose must end and must also begin.

Revolutionary consequences are bound to follow a higher and more fundamental purpose. Like Abraham as he journeyed before God, you will live a life of trust in the divine providence. But unlike those who comply with the universal human desire to parade virtue and good deeds in order to receive recognition and honor, you will comply with Jesus' recommendation to do good in secret, for "your Father who sees in secret will reward you" (Mt 6:18). When you do that, and when you revise your priorities, God will send you to others, advising you to "Let your light shine before others, so that they may see your good works and give glory to your Father in heaven" (Mt 6:14). Then, whatever you do becomes a ministry, the transforming work of God.

Why do so many people have an identity crisis? One of the reasons they are so confused about who they are and their real purpose is that they don't remember the theology of their baptism. Their baptism should remind them that they are children of God and that they have a God-given mission to spread the Good News to all people.

Everyone is called to the fundamental and higher purpose of being a child of God through faith in Jesus Christ (see 1 Jn 3:1). We do this by identifying with Christ and with others (see Heb 3:1; Gal 1:6–9), by developing holiness in everything we do (see 1 Pet 1:15; 3:9), and by serving God and others through everything we do and say (see 1 Pet 2:9–10, 21).

Realizing that you are a child of God—your oldest, deepest, and most basic identity—makes you realize at the same time that God did not send you here without a special purpose for your life, which is part of God's plan for the world as well.

We seem directed to start at the top of the ladder, not at the bottom as conventional wisdom tends to believe. Maybe this is a more efficient way for looking at things and changing them; focusing on the final goal gives life and energizes the whole process.

We have a divine mission to co-create the world, and we do this through our everyday choices. Thus we must be sure that every one of these choices, every commitment and every action, contributes to advancing our evolution as individual souls, which will contribute, in turn, to the overall evolution of human consciousness.

Because we exist within the universal field of consciousness, we affect this field through our thoughts, intentions, and visions. People who are happy, for example, have found a purpose that best uses their strengths. They feel a sense of being at home in what they do because they are participating in building the kingdom of God. In the kingdom of God, there is no unemployment. There, no one is allowed to just sit by idly. There, you are busy being holy.

Call to Holiness

Lao Tzu, the famous Chinese philosopher of the sixth century BC, believed that the most difficult thing to do was to be. How true and how important it is "to be," especially in the context of spiritual life.

If our purpose is to make the world holy by being true children of God—again, this is what our fundamental purpose comes down to—the first step toward that noble goal is to be holy ourselves. God wants to change the world not necessarily through miracles, but certainly through each one of us by dwelling in us and radiating through the grace and gift of our holiness.

Throughout the Bible, Christian tradition, and the works of theologians and spiritual authors, one is struck by the urgent call to holiness. But holiness first should be understood as a special gift from God, a grace that permeates our soul and transforms our life. A special gift from God does not mean that it is the monopoly of certain people. Holiness is available to anyone, whatever their the status of life, occupation, or circumstances. The Second Vatican Council is emphatic in this regard:

> The followers of Christ are called by God, not according to their accomplishments, but according to his own purpose and grace. They are justified in the Lord Jesus, and through baptism sought in faith they truly become sons of God and sharers in the divine nature. In this way they are really made holy. Then, too, by God's gifts they must hold on to and complete in their lives this holiness which they have received.
>
> *Lumen Gentium*, 40

Both the laity and clergy are, without distinction, called to the same heights of holiness:

In the various types and duties of life, one and the same holiness is cultivated by all who are moved by the Spirit of God....All of Christ's faithful, whatever be the conditions, duties, and circumstances of their lives, will grow in holiness day by day through these very situations, if they accept all of them with faith from the hand of their heavenly Father, and if they cooperate with the divine will by showing every man through their earthly activities the love with which God has loved the world.

All of Christ's followers, therefore, are invited and bound to pursue holiness and the perfect fulfillment of their proper state.

Lumen Gentium, 41–2

Why is this general call for holiness so important? It is so, not only for the good reason of salvation, but also because holiness and mission (another aspect of our fundamental purpose) are correlative. Growth in holiness brings with it the urge to witness to the Good News. By receiving the grace of holiness, one allows the Holy Spirit to radiate the energy for creating a reality in the spirit according to the values of the gospel.

The Second Vatican Council reminds us that "Missionary activity wells up from the Church's

innermost nature…[and] bears witness to her sanc-
tity while spreading and promoting it" (*Ad Gentes*, 6).
Holiness and mission (or evangelization) have this
absolute correlation because all of us are called to
union with the Christ who said, "And I, when I am
lifted up from the earth, will draw all people to
myself" (Jn 12:32).

Focusing on God alone compels us
to revise our values and readjust our
priorities. It compels every one of us
to face questions such as: What is my
true nature? Why am I here? What
are my real values? What do I truly
care about?

> Focusing
> on God
> alone
> compels us
> to revise
> our values.

There is no substitute for honestly
answering these questions and for
knowing what truly matters to us.
We may find solutions for the problems that are
bound to occur in life, but finding solutions does not
necessarily bring the happiness and fulfilled life we
long for. We most find fulfillment when our lives
rotate around a clear axis of the true values of the
gospel that lead to the communion with God when
we are able to say genuinely with Paul, "It is no longer
I who live, but it is Christ who lives in me" (Gal 2:20).

This is what fundamental purpose is and does. This is what saints do. They are anchored in God. God is the center around which their life rotates. This is why we need even more saints today. We need them more than we need advanced technologies, cunning politicians, or eloquent preachers. Our age needs them because they put before us pressing invitations to follow our fundamental purpose in life.

The only worthy response to this fundamental purpose, which is the inner call of God's image and grace, is a free, deliberate, and personal commitment. Pope John XXIII wrote in his book *Journal of a Soul*: "If I really wish to become good in every respect, fully to realize my ideals and be of use to the cause of Christ and the Church, I must at all costs make myself holy."

He further wrote: "Everyone calls me 'Holy Father,' and holy I must and will be." This is commitment.

> When you realize your fundamental purpose, expect the miracle of healing.

When you realize your fundamental purpose, expect the miracle of healing for yourself, for those who are in immediate contact with you, and for those who are removed from your surroundings. Indeed, your very relationship with everyone and everything is healed. Pope John XXIII wrote: "If all men are in the likeness of God, why should I not love them all, why should I despise them? Should I not rather revere them? This is the reflection which must hold me back from in any way offending against my brothers, for I must remember that they are all made in the image of God and that perhaps their souls are more beautiful and dearer to God than my own."

This is God's purpose for us. It is a faith purpose that is focused on God's life-changing plan. We can have what we can see. It is in God's plan to be this way. We are unfinished people. We are God's living enterprise.

Does it make a difference that you exist? Of course it does, precisely because you are one of a kind. You are an original. You are essential. You are an unprecedented event, and, at the same time, a universal representative of creation. You are an expression of the creation. You are a pilgrim of the future. You are God's living icon. You can, through your purpose and God's help, choose to redesign the package you call "me," your world, and the world at large.

When we contribute to the divine purpose, we live for a larger goal. We realize that our actions matter, and that we share in the redemption of the world and in the creation of a new world with a new world order. Indeed,

God designed humans for an awesome purpose.

After a long-time struggle with her shadows and wounds of the past, Loretta, whose story I mentioned in chapter one, decided to redesign her "me" package. She accepted the fact that she was a true child of God, surrendered totally to the divine providence, and aligned her will to the will of God, totally and decisively.

Loretta's thirst for the Infinite is overwhelming: an existential longing keeps deepening in her heart, and any other satisfaction seems secondary. Her purpose now is clear: to become as holy as she can. Her determination is firm: "Do something beautiful for God," as Mother Teresa would say. Her immediate duty is forthright: to heal herself completely and help to heal the members of her family, her friends, and all those who come in contact with her. Loretta is aware of the fact that she has been sent to her family for a purpose. Now she wants to fulfill her mission, as she was doing all along, without being aware of it. Now, more than ever before, her generous heart is eager to help others grow and bloom. Now, she radiates deep joy—the joy of discovering a meaningful life.

By giving meaning to life, fundamental purpose is one of the best medicines that exist.

Existential Longing

In his *Confessions*, St. Augustine wrote this memorable line: "O Lord…You have made us for yourself, and our hearts are restless until they can find peace in you." Augustine described with the utmost accuracy the spiritual thirst and existential longing for being what God wants us to be, and for growing according to God's image and likeness (see Gen 1:26).

Such a longing is at the heart of being human. It is a longing that will remain in the hearts of human beings until the time God's image reaches its full fruition. Thus, our answer to the question, "What fulfills the purpose for which I was made?" is of critical importance. If we fail to provide a positive answer, not only are we not happy, but we also tend to destroy ourselves as human beings.

> You can, through your purpose and God's help, choose to redesign the package you call "me."

Since the beginning of time, thirst has been digging deep in the human heart. Who in human history, and who among us now, at one point or another in their lives, did not cry out as the psalmist did?

As a deer longs for flowing streams,
so my soul longs for you,
O God.
My soul thirsts for God,
for the living God.
When shall I come and behold
the face of God?

Deep calls to deep
at the thunder of your cataracts;
all your waves and your billows
have gone over me.
By day the Lord commands his
steadfast love,
and at night his song is with me,
a prayer to the God of my life.

Psalm 42:1–2, 7–8

This is a thirst that only God—no one and nothing else—can extinguish. God promised, "To the thirsty I will give water as a gift from the spring of the water of life" (Rev 21:6).

It is remarkable how we always want to stretch out. We want more of everything—be it material or not so material—until we "possess" the Infinite that makes all other possessions futile and illusory.

Fundamental purpose is essential for the understanding of what being human is all about. No Christian anthropology is possible without the original blessings of Adam and Eve who were made in God's image, an image that remained permanent and immutable. We are ontologically theological beings. Our ontology is iconic. And we are eschatologically theological. Our final destination is also our beginning. Our God is our Alpha and Omega; our destiny is permeated by deifying grace.

> By giving meaning to life, purpose is one of the best medicines that exist.

God destined us to be conformed to God's own image and likeness. We sinned. And now God's purpose is to restore in us this image through sanctification.

To grasp the depth of our destiny will certainly make a difference in how we live our lives. We will realize that we, each one of us, have eternal infinite value in the eyes of God, and that we have a duty to heal, help each other to heal, and form a harmonious unity which embraces diversity. To mirror God empowers us to show love and respect for others and for all creation. The more we yield to the image of God, the more love will be the essence of our nature and of what we do to each other.

How much easier it would be to deal with the daily problems we face, if we could have the assurance that our life is part of a grand divine plan. This is exactly what St. Paul conveys to the Romans and to us: "We know that all things work together for good for those who love God, who are called according to his purpose….If God is for us, who is against us? He who did not withhold his own Son, but gave him up for all of us, will he not with him also give us everything else?" (Rom 8:28, 31–32)

FOR YOUR REFLECTION & RESPONSE

1. Can you introduce yourself to others without referring to what you do for living? Do you usually do something just for the fun of it or do you usually do things with a production-minded attitude? Have you ever considered working for a cause? What will be your answer at the gates of heaven to the question "Who are you?"

Do you feel that your life is filled with grace? Have you ever encountered grace in unlikely places and uncertain times? Have you ever felt a mysterious sense of the presence of "Someone" in your life, who is in your company in good and bad times?

2. Can you name five people who have made a difference in your life? What were the characteristics in them that struck a chord in your soul? Can you name five events in your life that left an important impact on your behavior? Do you know why these events were so influential?

3. If your life were a book, what title would you give it? Do you have a desire to go beyond success to significance? Do you listen to God's calling for you? Do you try to decipher the puzzles of your own life by yourself or do you live with your eye upon God, living the commandments and reflecting the values of the gospel?

4. Are you influenced by our consumer society when you have to determine what your real wants and needs are? Do you do what you do for a certain cause you have in mind and heart, and above all for God's sake? What is the "philosopher's stone" that you think will turn your life into gold?

5. Is your faith relevant in your home as well as at your places of work and recreation? Do you have a purpose that fuels your passion for acting as "salt" and "light" for the world (Mt 5:13–14)? Would Jesus be able to say of you what he said of the woman who bathed his feet with her tears (see Lk 7:37–50)? Do you feel prepared, like St. Thérèse of Lisieux, to "have no other desire except to love Jesus unto folly" and say: "I can no longer ask for anything with fervor except the accomplishment of God's will in my soul without any creature being able to set obstacles in the way"?

AFFIRMATION

Repeat this several times a day.

I must and will be holy.

PRAYER

Dear Lord, I pray that my inward eyes be illuminated, so I can see your image in the depth of my soul and heart. I pray so I can clearly picture your calling for me and discern all that you have in store for my life on this earth.

I pray so I can visualize my fundamental purpose and see its connection to your universal plan.

I pray that my vision won't become blurred and shortsighted because of the few successes I might have had, when I am supposed to focus on you. I pray that you deliver me from the prison of my past, from my mistakes and many wounds, and focus on a redemptive present and faith-filled future.

I pray that you make me healthy, happy, and holy. I pray that you make me an instrument through which your divine life flows freely to the world. I pray that the love and peace you surround me with help me to be more aware of the growing sense that everything in my life is unfolding according to your purpose—my fundamental purpose.

And, with the deepest gratitude, I thank you for the joy in my heart and the meaningfulness in my life— you are my joy, you are the meaning of my life. Amen.

It does not matter much where you start. What really matters is where you finish. It is at the end that your fortune finishes, but it is also there that it begins. Your purpose is the great magnet that attracts the circumstances that make you what you are.

Having a purpose and striving to achieve it helps us realize an abundant life of health, wealth, and well-being.

A life purpose brings the essential elements to answer the most serious questions of life. We will possess the secrets of: What is my life really all about? What is its meaning? What is true fulfillment? Do I want to be part of something larger than myself? Do I have something unique to share with the world? Where am I headed? Does it make a difference that I exist?

A purpose, by stirring passion and love to something greater than ourselves, and by bestowing meaning on what we do, spares us from existential frustration, restlessness, boredom, depression, or, in some cases, more severe illnesses. A purpose makes us live a life worth living, and brings us deep joy and satisfaction.

> To mirror God empowers us to show love and respect for others and for all creation.

God gave each one of us a certain number of gifts. What do we do with them? God has for each one of us a special calling. How do we respond to it? God has a global purpose for the creation. Do we align ourselves to it? We are God's children. How can we still have identity problems? God calls us through our giftedness, family heritage, and life opportunities. How do we miss them? God calls us to be who we are. Why do we want to be someone else? God gave us a name. Do we live up to its significance?

When God, in the Hebrew scripture, gave new names to "Abram" and "Jacob" to become "Abraham"

(Gen 17:5) and "Israel" (Gen 32:28), they were marked in a particular way by God's grace and power to perform a certain mission. The new names mean, besides a deepened intimacy with God, the fulfillment of God's purpose for that person and for what that person is going to do.

Similarly, everyone has figuratively a new name, but we cannot recognize it until we are ready to hear it and to know our own purpose, which is God's purpose for us. Then, it seems that we have always known who we are. And being who we are is our best contribution to our immediate community as well as to the world at large.

In each one of us, there is a deeper flow of life that underlies our day-to-day events. We must discern and recognize this fundamental aspect of our lives. We may take hold of it when we are quiet and alone and absorbed by a meditative prayer, or we can detect it in the midst of some animated discussions and inspired guidance. In any case, checking deep inside is a critical step that helps align all that we do in, and of, our life with who and what we are meant to be.

When you align yourself with the deepest and most solid ground of your being, you create what you want, without falling victim to your circumstances.

As a consequence, most of the difficulties of your life situation, and perhaps what you even considered impasses, are no longer important issues for you, and they may even disappear. And naturally, your different physical, mental, emotional, and spiritual forces start again to work in harmony. You become a fully integrated being—a holy being.

Furthermore, the fundamental purpose—our deepest calling—frees us. It enables us to focus on what really matters—Someone or something larger than ourselves. By doing so, we become free from all the things that are not related to the "only one thing" (Lk 10:42) that is necessary, and we create the field of consciousness that gives birth to a new and transformed reality.

A transformation in mind, heart, and spirit—a new identity in Christ—is the most important and enduring healing of all, indeed.